AF288776

PROJECT METROPOLITAN

PROJECT METROPOLITAN

Bibliografische Information der deutschen Nationalbibliothek
Die deutsche Nationalbibliothek verzeichnet diese Publikation
in der deutschen Nationalbibliografie; detaillierte bibliografische
Daten sind im Internet über http://www.d-nb.de abrufbar

Umschlaggestaltung und Satz
Tobias Meyer (www.tobsemeyer.de)
Schrift: Delicious by Jos Buivenga (www.exljbris.com)

Fotografien
Ilja M. Inesz & Alex Khan (Seite 65–72, 76)
Tearstain (Seite 73–75, 77)

Illustrationen
Tobias Meyer (Umschlag, Seite 3, Seite 33–37)

Herstellung und Verlag
Books on Demand GmBH, Norderstedt

Das Copyright auf die Texte liegt bei den Autorinnen
und Autoren, für diese Ausgabe beim Herausgeber

© 2010

Mit freundlicher Förderung der

Stadt Braunschweig

ISBN: 978-3-8391-3863-2

Printed in Germany

LIST OF AUTHORS

ALEX KHAN [AK]
English Seminar; TU Carolo Wilhelmina, Brunswick

BERNT PATZE [BP]
Herbert Mehrtens
History Seminar; TU Carolo Wilhelmina, Brunswick

ILJA M. INESZ [II]
English Seminar; TU Carolo Wilhelmina, Brunswick

MARA KITTEL [MK]
English Seminar; TU Carolo Wilhelmina, Brunswick

SATYRICUS [ST]
Alexej Artreich
German Seminar; TU Carolo Wilhelmina, Brunswick

TEARSTAIN [TS]
Bjoern Schubert
American Studies; Humboldt University, Berlin

TILL KINZEL [TK]
English Seminar; TU Carolo Wilhelmina, Brunswick

CONTENT

FOREWORD

For the most part we do not first see and then define, we define first and then see. In the great blooming, buzzy confusion of the outer world we pick out what our culture already defined for us, and we tend to perceive that which we have picked out in the form stereotyped for us by our culture.

WALTER LIPPMANN [1922]: *Public Opinion*

The main objective of this work has been to delve into different aspects of metropolitan life and the different ways of perceiving familiar places. Rooted in and surrounded by our personal everyday settings we have – in fact – become accustomed to their structures; their frames have become habitualised. Often it is this [involuntary] habitualisation of concepts which hinders us from acknowledging the uniqueness of the metropolitan space in time.

Our experiences depend on motives of moving within quite common frames. Once we leave these supposedly familiar surroundings, [our] concepts shatter: visits to rural areas as well as rambling through other metropolitan areas reframe our perceptions. Alongside the change of perspective comes a change of vision, a development that is part of the perpetual cycle or entering a foreign space and becoming accustomed to it by means of structuring the new perceptions according to preset principles based on our previous experiences.

In the beginning the project was planned and structured with a strictly poetic agenda. Since then, new participants gave their 'thumbs up' for their contributions from which followed the restructuring and redefinition of the original concept.

The project received a new overall perspective as the horizon of experience broadened, allowing for a range of other perceptions of metropolitan spaces. Assembling the different impressions, perceptions and pieces by the contributing artists and authors over the period of 18 months resembled the creation of a mosaic. Taken together – and reassembled – these snapshots and momentary impressions of different cities have created a wholly new space that seems to be more honest and closer to the true face of any metropolis. The group consists of seven writers and one student of art & photography – all with their personal accounts of foreign yet strangely familiar grounds.

Instead of restricting ourselves to poetry, we have opened up for prose thus closing a gap, providing room for more elaborate ideas. Furthermore, the photos or collages serve as a loose commentary.

I am indebted to the Abteilung Kulturinstitut of the City of Braunschweig for their ample support without which this publication would not have been possible. I thank all contributors for their ideas: Alex Khan, Mara Kittel, Herbert Mehrtens, Till Kinzel, Alexej Artreich and Bjoern Schubert. Furthermore, the realisation of the project would not have been possible without the effort of Tobias Meyer, who not only designed the cover but took over responsibility for the layout of the book. Special thanks go to my sweet Natalia for her perpetual encouragement and effort put into the first exhibition and read-in.

Many thanks to Prof. Dr. Franz Meier, managing director of the English Seminar at the TU Braunschweig, for his support of previous projects and much interest in this work, Dr. Lawrence Guntner and Dr. Till Kinzel for their interest in this work and their readiness to help during the process of editing. Last but not least I thank Mara Kittel for her editing, advice and active participation
ILJA.M.INESZ, Brunswick, December 31st, 2009

METROPOLITAN I [II 2005]

arisen towers stand statue-like,
take away space and give meaning to life,
claim a huge intensity
from the brightening sun – day-light,
keep away the shining gleam from its creators.

the traitors of the past and presence
live futurous rememberance
erected, shape and yet still plan
steel-boned elevating bridges up to heaven
with a mass of human ants circling around them.

infrastructural competetiveness points,
forces the people's gaze onto the streets
and intersections which remain,
belong to them unloved and in Hades
until some Orpheus plays the flute

and destroys these civilisationary necklaces,
distracted by over-dimensioned flies.
but they will be restored and will symbolize
a new-shaped adapted modernism
named after Shelleyan Frankensteins.

BRICKS [ST 2009]

no broken bricks
just steel and glass
in grief relieved
to their brothers
abroad
yet still the old ones
will claim their tribute
to the fragment

METROPOLITAN III [II 2006]

monoliths ascend
representative visions
of transcending truths
scarcely sustained
by the memories of time,
parcouring individualistically pulsating veins
as framing hindering hurdles
never to be overcome

DUST [MK 2009]

the air
full of dust
that chokes
the young ones,
kills
the old
and slowly
      slowly
           stifles
                the last
breath
of the last
emerald soul
that longs
to see the
stars
it has never known.

METROPOLITAN VI [II 2010]

everyday reading: press and release

scribes eyewitness bombs,
masses not in tombs,
troups marching through the street,
exiled heirs
and presidents overthrown

                               sources cited

incoming files
ideas of logic
transferred and balanced
matching purchased pictures
contextualising dramatic reason

                               bomb ignited

flying letters
herald tribute,
assemble lines
to defunct interpretation,
shared values
and manufactured consent.

                               blog-world thinking about

                               action but in words.

METROPOLITAN IV [II 2006]

state-owned people's factories
spit liquid waste into sewaged sombre rivers,
snorting chimneys fill a city-covering pall
of smoky hazardous haze
veiling past modernity's promising future.

productivity orders from state's planning committee
bend weakened backs
of blue collar work force,
stumbling along between age old
ravines of shimmering red-bricked gaping flesh
laid bare by weathered torn-down rendering
arduously fixed by dried-out crumbed mortar.

    hazy veils immerse people and obscure suns
    into shades of ochre and grey

open swung heavy wooden doors
click creakingly shut;
workers take refuge near ovens' enchanting warmth
burning on broken promises' firing heat,
trying to forget acid sounds
of lodging trucks and lorries
bumping over rough roads,
silently listening to citys's bustle
let in through windows' distorted frames.

    sooty rain dusts white-washed linen.

OPINIONATED PIDGEON [MK 2009]

Rats
of the air
you   call us.
Rats
of the world
we call you who spread
the plague wherever you go
and build your stinking cities
wherever you settle. Loud, deadly, horrible
places with crippling traps
on your window sills.
We don't like
you
either.
But we're many and your food is good!

DREAM [ST 2009]

here rests
on conquered beaches
of the organic
regaining their pillars
of paradise
the dream of a plastic bag
stolen from the wind
caught from the fence
that burdens
to separate the opponent
contracts in a while
inhales, exhales
abandonments

WALKING DOWN IN TOWN AT DUSK

[TS 2008]

This ache

        Pauses

                To beat

                           {My

heart}

as the streets bleed out her name.

METROPOLITAN XIII [II 2007]

crimson-lit facades
billow down laughters,
moans and cries –
lies fly down
and earth me

laterns light the leafed hallways
whistling

bridges' bows
echo
me

THE RIVER [TS 2006]

How can somebody so beautiful be so sad?
Her tears form a silent trail down her bare breasts
      like a shadow she hides from life
my silent beauty, an eternal child
imprisons herself in her rented cave.
      But I am wrong to tell her that.
To tell anyone how to lead their life
or how to be in love with their own life
not even me, who holds her close and loves her so.
Only she sees the world thru her own eyes.
I know I cannot ever help her find her way.
My words just make it so much worse
      while her rivers keep flowing
I slowly close the door
for this moment in time
pray for future days ahead
      to find a way
      to share my life with her.

WITHOUT TITLE [TK 1995]

The screen is flickering
and sounds, queer, queer,
quite queer
come from within
and colours come
and colours go
and catch the eye,
and revolutions through the walls are to be heard
the mumbling of the washing-machine
while cars go by
12 GMT, and, this is London,
the world
breaks in upon me,
it is the tyranny
of new and newer and still newer things

the biting smell of floor wax
drifts in the nostrils
biting sharp, I biting back to no avail
and therefore flee the room
out in the wind
out, out
and there the wind
catches the leaves
both of the trees
and of the book
I hold with fingertips and thumb,
the leaves drift through the air,
hurled upwards and then down again,
and I into the book,
the wind blows past me.

METROPOLITAN XIV [II 2007]

The doors, the frames, the sills,
the glazen eye distills
the fired wood, the broken dawn
and me, below them, drawn

to their hiding, biting glaze
of single lighted heads
that match the shadows
to its blaze.

A heap of wind intrudes,
the candle's light preludes –

bound to it the shadows shuffle
in heaps and heaves the lovers muffle.

THE LOOKING GLASS [TS 2006]

I remember a day
sparkling rain upon
the pegoda
mini sanctions of drops
upon rocks
transcending
invisible walls
within.

Her window sill
I climbed
beyond the looking glass
rat race order
to find the culprit.

My belly on the wooden floor
crestfallen I wake
with a jolt
inherit a footing
to adore.

HOME [II 2006]

impenetrable paper walls

inked

with passionate love and longing

secluding

awkwardness and secret thoughts.

CRYSTAL CITY [MK 2009]

In the hallway
on the lift
across the street from the historical building
on the way to the trash bin
on the bus
in the bank
in the restaurant
feeding pigeons in the park
on the market
public toilet
shopping aisle
Big Brother is watching
Oh, Brave New World
Hey you, yeah, the tall one with the black leather jacket. The fag
goes into the bin – and Louise says get your hair cut. Thank you.

SURVEILLANCE [II 2005]

I am being watched
as I set one foot
before the other –
smooth and silently
to avoid any self-made noise
though there are many
from the trafficking around

but still my heart
faints from the unbearable
feeling of being looked at
or better: 'being
looked down at'
numerous times and sometimes
without knowledge

around the corner –
in an instant – I see
what I already
knew: cams on almost
every building, not hovering
in the sky, not ready to dive,
but no less threatening:

electronic lensed eyes
of a system that causes

an induced feeling of
reduced freedom
just by following the
suspicious, following any threat to the system.

I go on – on screen as well –
lost in my tracks,
pull out a map and
circle standing still around;
a police car passes by,
I am watched at,
but feel cared for
and finally secure.

METROPOLITAN V [II 2005–2006]

on body bags facading
mindless murmuring machines
their minute erectors
attach antennae,
broadcast bigoted pragmatism
screaching scorching life on screen

modern media minstrels bend
minds into mirage views,
turn remote controlling minds
into remote-controlled
news-flash minions
listening to leaders living their lies

state's re-run statements
induce minions into believing
invoked mendacity,
extenuated reality,
trusting thrusted-into-them ideas,
defending implanted agendas - not their own

    power's treason
    transmittingly replaces
    human reason

    replaces human reason

RED LIGHT [MK 2009]

Red Light
City Night
Pseudo-silk kimono
And a cheap
Pack of cigarettes
Besides
The dirty green
On the bed-
Side table.
Whore,
Temptress,
Lady of the Evening!
Happy Mother's Day,
Mommy!
Sister,
Could you?
No!
But she's only small.
Exhausts exhaust the exhausted
Child
Blue lights
Sirens howl
No insurance will pay
Except for a coffin.
The city doesn't
Care
When its lights
Go   Out.

THE UNNAMED [II 2009]

The unnamed linger
near the entrance hall
obvious statements
in kinky lingerie,
making fun of the boys
with unsatisfied hard-ons,
grunty their voices,
their eyes growing wild,

itchy bulges awaiting
to dump the load
into these rent-out bodies:
servile squirming cans of trash.
Rats just wave
catish glimpses and
chariot smiles
waiting for a blood-barred knife,
bloody stains and scratches,
body-count marks.

unyielding screams,
brutal swings,
hefty stabs run into
ripped-through flesh,
eyes lashed deep
tear from blood,
wounds remain
instead of sight.

Aimed at her
treasuring treacherous soul
all-too-mighty forty stabs
butcher-knife the element
of crime,
strip off the beauty
from the beauty's
stripped-off body.

Blood runs out
the severed sewer,
splashes onto the floor
through open gutters
and onto her,
lying there.#

People heard
her feverish screams,
her blazing eyes unseen,
the past now just
and from the blast
it just remains
one ten page file.

Ankle straps
now trap him down,
syringes stitch his craze:
recast life
within cosy walls
prevent another
diabolical furore.

BEGGAR BAILEY [II 2009]

beggar bailey drinking scotch
sleeps in a tent at hillwood park
the warmth he feels comes from within
bought from a few dimes
being tossed at him
begging in the streets

Americans dream
while homeless scream
from sickness and despair
the rags and the bowler
made like a fowler
and the spring
brings a break to being,
rain gushes its way
what ways are not seen

the blinks and the stares,
bought by the riches
bedazzle the eyes
cuddled muds not seen
just on screen in hollied word
on flickering screen

BEYOND BELIEF [TS 2004]

i am in the center
not of the universe
but out in the springtime park
i listen to the surrounding sounds
everyone i see keeps going around
me sitting out here on my own
the first passerby's
after a long lonesome while
are two old ladies
very busy talking to each other
with two cute doggies
very busy following both of them
i grab for my can of green pulp tea
taste for Sunny, a breeze underneath
those bare old trees i feel so free
for a single moment lets me unwind
till they pass by me a second time
a déja-vu with the same scenery!
isn't it funny?
we all keep walking in circles
over and over
i wish i could just let myself take off for a breakout
welcome to nowhere at black rock and make out
burn down the man on the salt white playa
burn my skin, burn aloud rock'n'rings on fire
leave my beloved circle of friends behind
travel my endless world full of possibilities
traverse those high above translucent skies
to walk into 8 Butterfields floating sky high
on a Ferris Wheel in Fourth of July's night sky

have breakfast at the 3rd coast oceans far away
next to a bald leading-edge star on his way
swim with five zwans in tune in the Paradiso
awake in white lost prairies, will ya let me go?
reach down to me for one last good-bye
leave the stage, hold your flying-V awry
i spill all the milk out before you go
cool as ice on trains with the flow
desperate to find some sorta truth
in one more glorious bliss of MUSE
but before i will unplug from you once and for all
unplug into me, my plug in baby lets me call
still wonder of who i am to you
for your love i will keep me true
within this full-of-life town
within my small own place
within my dream and woes
within your false love taste.

tearstained i jolly joke my heart out
to you hot dark eyed phantom-child
restless i am before i go to rock out
to seek what i won't ever find
out here in the park.

MANHATTAN MEMORIES [BP 2009]

One day I walked down Columbus Avenue
All the way
Nothing happened
Another day I walked down Columbus Avenue
And stopped by a shop
Bought a Danish pocket watch
For fifty bucks
It stayed with me
Company for many years
At some point of time it stopped
The repair cost fifty Euros
Soon after it had its ultimate stop: 4:29 pm

I don't remember what happened after buying the watch
But Columbus Circle is a place I will never forget
I don't know why
Maybe because it is on the corner of Central Park
Where I once heard a young woman tell funny stories
Of little Hermes and Zeus
It took some time
To understand the names
Classic Greek in Manhattan is strange
My teacher in public speaking years before
Talking about Greek drama
Said: you rippe dese pants and you'll get a spanking.

New Yorkers told me
To have twenty dollars with me
In case of a holdup
A young woman held me up
Near Times Square
Begging in a German accent
For some change
In a café across the street
She talked about Manhattan in deep sea metaphor
Showed me a book about oceanography from her handbag
And a photo of her small room and her cat
There went my twenty bucks

On a stormy day
I learned that skyscrapers kill umbrellas
Crippled specimen were all around
My Manhattan friend had already warned me
He had also taken me to Christopher Street
To a warm and friendly place where I sang along
And a dark leather place were I felt cold
On that cold and rainy Sunday
I walked down deserted First Avenue
And spotted a black steaming hemisphere
An Igloo built from reconstructed umbrellas
On an outlet of the Manhattan heating system

It might have been around 4.30 pm
Reminding me of Tsorróh Woldén
(As a Parisian bookseller called into the back of the shop
When I asked for the book, some time in the afternoon)

CHARITY BURNING [II 2009]

charity is burning in the streets
fire is lit
and the homeless bleeds
from leaks in his soul
and a wasted life.

the cars pass by and the strangers freeze
cold wind blowing
no use pray to jees'
as the hope for home
lies in a bag.

just found rags made for a living
and shivering stitches
from knitting hands
split up nails

it is the town in despair
that quietly lies
distorted screams from a beat up life
out in the streets where the gangs
crate off the living.

in dismembering colds and winds
blow in heaps,
in December the blue Ray
is freezing
slowly

charity comes, one time, a meal
served by a star, everyone mutters
when stuffed files out,
into the maze of his mind
and the gringe.

THE BEATING [II 2009]

too drunk to watch out
one tumbles across the streets
into the arms of a gang
out for a fight.

too drunk to watch out
the first hits
and one falls
down with the head on the floor

blood stains the street
the lights go off
dreams begin to float through the mind
agony does not subside

nor do the breaths
the breast
distorted extremities
and bones still splinter

organs refuse their work
the breath subsides
just room for
silenced screams

down the street
a blue light comes
the gangsters flee
the dreams go on – bad dreams.

the white cell paves its way
through crowded lanes
the dreams filled with sirens singing

hands grab and fondle between
the clothes, cut the cloth
more blood emerges from the drowning flesh

all over bruises,
marks of the night drinking,
still there – dreams.

CITY TOUR [ST 2009]

And where the flesh crawls
you ought to stay calm
and in the sideways
those open cabins of the
architectured rocks

And where the blood and bonestream rolls
you shall not tint your
pale hands palm
frantically mistaken
to touch life in those waters

Take the grey and blue
alignments
of the iron sheets
to guide you
to isolation

PORTOMENTALI DRIVEN [BP 2009]

From hamburg to berlin to paris to rome to budapest
From hamlin to berris to pameburg to rolin pudabest
From hamberl to da pestburg in burisda paromin
From be to harm to purrling aribus to depastrome
From bure ham to parlin bader urgis me to stop
Metropolitan nervid

LIVERPOOL – DOCKS [II 2005]

bar and canteen;
strongbow,
breast of corn-stuffed chicken,
garlic bread,
pudding,
cappuccino.

between the courses
enough time to watch
silently
for I am on my own –
nothing to say
except to order.

the smoothly blastering sound
of backgrounded music
massages my ears and rubs
melodies deep
into my wavering
attention-full sourround glancing mind.

at stroke of twelve a lonesome guy,
rejecting ordered food to eat it later
after having finished the newspaper
and making phone calls –
short haired, spiked high,
a suit that does not suit him well,

a clown to me,
embarrassment to the cute blonde waitress
who just takes back the dishes
just to serve them again –
he, too, is sitting all alone but
has no more in common with me.

at one – two girls
at the far end corner
near the bar's high end windows
dressed to hide
from apparently lacking coldness,
hair floating half-way down their backs

just as I like it – I like them –
stuck to their drinks –
nothing to eat –
and their digital cameras,
zooming in
their girlish giggles.

at half two
two businessmen
that at least seem
to enjoy their dinner,
but that is what I see:
I do not share their tastes,

neither do I speak out
their thoughts reflected in their faces
and important letters in their suitcases
with locks to shut and keep them closed –
confidentiality at stake,
importance just a missed take;

impostered 'self-made' men
that take refuge in showing off,
ordering wine and steak,
golden watches round their wrists;
over-rating their importance and under-valuing –
they surely should watch out.

I look at the clock,
watch a minute more
forks and cuts,
sip my last drop and would like to pay
for the opulent meal
and the friendliness of the smiling waitress,

a girl stepping in and out of my life.
serving – in time
my time alone
I spent
and leave –
a tip.

COFFEE # 1 [TS 2006]

tenderly chatter
flattery laughter
colorfull eyes
meet in the rise
coffee steams crystalize
in finest gourmet taste
the music plays
the soul fades
it all comes into place
from the endless race
coffee stains on newspaper heads
fags in adds
a book full of letters
from old hipster Jack
"isn't he from my days?"
desire manifests
in memorized fragments
of mere snapshot reflections
rushing in and out
between the sunshowers
and drops
"here you can have all four seasons in one day!"
it never stops.

THE NUTCRACKER [TS 2004]

love does not exist for me
because i don't seem to exist
just a projection in my mind
of what you see in me

i can't look at the crooked reflection of myself
on the steps down the red carpet Palais staircase
i appear and i disappear from various sceneries
old ghost lovers seem to gaze right through me

From the fourth row we watched the parade of the ballet last
night graceful dancers spinning upside down around – in fake
snow
so beautiful told – fairy tales.

lost in thoughts
i lost my sense of time
the days fade from me
without a trace.

RAVE O NETTES [II 2009–2010]

blue and red
change in beat
rhythm-sticked humming
giving the lead
to bound-in lyrics
not to discern.
upright pose,
her eyes
leak prose
to guitar chords

diachronically beating.
flashing lights to liquid ceiling
crystal globe
no heart-cry feeling
glaciers melting
in the glass.
swinging hips
two rows ahead
mad-for-tongue lips
kissing like mad.

Lip gloss smeared
and wet shirt hosed
inte the "lido" tonight:
areolas exposed –
and a friend is riding high sky

THE PLAN [TS 2005]

We come in, sit down, order food
Hot coffee along with ham and cheese toastie
5,65 – 'Oh, and tap water, please!'
Pull out my book
Beat down to your soul
Now reading a letter
A piece of art
A piece straight from the heart
Held in my bare hands
Seems forever waiting for reply
Time is meaningless, is it?
But why do loved ones have to go and we are still here?
A series of initial moments of surprise, discovery, the mystery of
'you and me'

Is not that what our given time is all about?
Outside, countless passerbys in November rain;
the same old winter blues
Inside, 'Rudolf The Red Nose Reindeer'; now on air

This dear old place is lit up by tea light candles
And elegant lanterns hanging down from the tall walls
Across these sky high windows an antique bookstore
An intimate atmosphere of breathing in history alive

"Oh...! This plate of food looks quite breathtaking
The French style coffee smells strongly heart fading
Mind me, I haven't eaten yet all day long
Suddenly I become so shattered shaken
While writing all this down, revising, eating

All at the same time!
I drop my knife, try to pick it up
Kick the small table instead
Spill half of my coffee milk
Across the letter and book
For a brief moment all looks are on me
My pale face must now be painted red
I guess, this wasn't my plan
Nevertheless I'll continue as before

Now we leave the scenery
We open the door
"See you tomorrow!"
Will we ever again at all?

NIGHT'S CLASH [II 2005]

"It's all about not where you go to
but who you go with."

"It's not about who you go with
but what you see!"

Looking up at night
a friend may see the black sky universe,
another one the street lamp
between us and the dark alley
branches of a tree.

Between the universe,
the sun and the street lamp
it's just us
breathing carbon-dioxide –
call it life.

DOWN AT ELLIOTT'S [TS 2005]

there are no stars

just candles and guitars

and a young moon glowing

behind the bar.

SENSUAL DRINK [AK 2009]

My lovely friend and cousin Tanya has always been making fun of me eating something tasty or drinking coffee. She says: *"You must not eat in public. It looks like you are having sex with your food."*

Well, to some extent she is right. I love coffee ... sometimes it happens ... I am sitting in a cafe in Germany, the weather as gloomy as the people living there and still ... something very familiar and warm is in the air. The smell comes slowly and fragmentary like the washed-out image of a picture, forgotten long ago but still so near and desirable. The spirals of the smell reach the nose frightened and shy. The brain starts searching for the answers in its cells and curved ways. The feeling of surprise and satisfaction is overcoming me like a sea wave. It is coffee!

My heart is beating faster and stronger, the world starts changing ... Paris, beginning of the 20th century ... sunset in spring ... pavilion ... a lady in white is sitting at a table. The picture is not sharp, not yet. It is rather like an impressionist painting. She is reading a novel by Alexandre Kuprin ... *Sulamith*. Well, it is me, travelling time. It is my world. Suddenly, something makes her stop reading. She lifts her eyes from the book and looks helplessly around ... reality? A dream? Yes, that is the reason ... it is crawling from the club café ... and whirling in the air like Coquette's hairdo ... no, now it is becoming stronger ... in a moment she will recognize it, but not yet ... now! It is coffee, Arabic coffee, so wonderful and precious like an oriental jewel ... where is the garçon ... the eyes of the lady stop wandering and sparkle. What time is it? How long ago did she place an order? Uneasiness is approaching. The lady is not reading any more. She is waiting for her coffee, her(!) coffee, waiting like a forty-year old woman trembling, waiting for her young lover. Steps behind ... a young Indian carrying a tray and with it ... coffee! Do not turn, do not look back ... the smell ... so strong and desirable ... .

"Your coffee madam."

"Yes, my coffee, thank you."

One sip, just one sip ... the passion of Solomon running through her veins ... the lady and her coffee ... becoming one ... .

Well, back in Germany! It is in fact me, making love with my coffee ... but that is not the most shameful thing. Imagine me, eating a corned-ice or banana! I think I would be able to write about that turning sixty.

It is a great feeling when you can speak about everything but can be accused of nothing. See you soon, my coffee. And now, I will go to my kitchen.

DUMPED [II 2006]

I

His mobile did not ring that often so he was surprised that somebody out there thought of him right now. *"Where is my mobile, where is it …?"* After half a dozen rings the alarming noise ceased. Not so the search for the phone presumably stuck under one of the several piles of notes covering the floor. It seems to be part of Murphy's law that when you are looking for something desperately, it is in the last place you would ever look, or in the place least expected. *"OK. Where did I put it?"* Remembrance reluctantly set down its heavy feet on his consciousness. *"Now – here we are!"* He remembered walking narrows at night time, heavy-cloaked to hide away from the cold. On his way he'd check his mobile several times, as if waiting for a call, and help an escape from his melancholy. But nobody had called. After loitering around in the park and arriving back home in his flat, he'd taken it out again and carelessly tossed it on the sideboard, where it crashed against the wall and landed on the floor. Against all odds it neither broke nor was it stepped on.

How disappointed he was, when he recognized it had been just another sms. How many people have his number? And how many actually wanted to get it? He could not think of anybody. The only friend he could think of without hesitation was Jérôme – a tall black-haired guy with a muscular body that spoke of his days as a committed swimmer. But his swimming days were gone. Not so his attractiveness. The women Jérôme met fell for him. How did he call it once? Acquiring carnal knowledge.

He opened the folder containing the newly arrived message. It read: *"Hey there. I know its quite out of the blu. How R U? Have to see you, talk to U. Hugs, Justine."* His mind was working like a mad-machine … She messaged me? Okay. She did. But ummmh – why? What's left to still have to talk about? Where did she get my number anyway? … Still absorbed in his musings another electronic telegram flashed the display, introduced by mobile's thunder. *"Me again. At UR place. 7pm? Justine".*

Well, it's around twelve now – so … seven hours to go … His day was shipwrecked. Too many scars, too many blunt knifes still stuck in his back. And still … What does she want??? … Along with daydreams, curses and daydreams again … Does she need help? Yeah. Right, now that she needs someone to help her over the tide I'm good enough. But – belle – you'd better wake up. Wake up from lucid phantasies and stick your feet through the door reading 'Emergence exit for elves and gnomes. Danger: Reality ahead. One Way. No turning back! … Reading it again: Justine.
     "JUSTINE FOR CHRISTSAKE! WHAT DO YOU WANT???" But there was no use in yelling at the mobile. Now I've got it. That limp deaf fucking bastard. He gave it away. JÉRÔME you moron, why did you give me away? *"DON'T YOU EVER LISTEN?"* I've been on the verge of forgetting – well, not forgetting, but, but numbed down a bit already. *"SHIT!!!"* And now she brings me about and appears back on board. Trust no one – I can't trust anybody! He almost choked on his hollering chuckles. "No one. Hehe – I know almost no one. I'm a one man show. Hadn't it been for the binge-drinking incident and Jérôme with his fucking jerk-ass care, I would be all alone, on my own and GODDAMMIT – solo … "

II

"Curious?" – From somewhere in the back of the café and bar the familiar voice greeted him. *"Women are a living 'curiosum', you know? One moment captivating caressing, the next minute raging harpies and ripping flesh."* Behind the bar Jérôme was filling up the fridges with new booze. He straightened up and sized up his flabbergasted friend.

"Come on. You know that I know, and another thing: you know that I won't tell. It's just like I've said, man. Each single one of them a living 'curiosum' … Have a drink! You look like you need one." Without waiting for reply he reached for a bottle of Vodka and poured a generous portion into a large tumbler.

"You are going to ask me whether I gave your number away. Damn straight! I did. And you guess that if she has your address – I'm the one to blame. Right again! So what?!"

"Jérôme – what the heck? She was the last person – living and dead – that I wanted to have my number or fucking address. It's over. I'm saturated, I'm stuffed – I've had enough."

"Listen, hey – hey! Don't turn away from me, enjoy your drink and look at me! Now listen, mr. dear fanciful and sobbing lonely hearts. Still strolling 'round???"

"What d'you mean?"

"Don't play stupid! What I mean is: strolling around, thinking too much, shutting yourself off from reality, shutting down and exercising just the basic skills – eating, drinking, sleeping, going for a piss and whatever else and – yeah – and drinking again. Another drink?"

Like a medic curing a patient with the right amount of antibiotics he poured in yet another fill and asked: *"Anything written lately?"*

"Just bits and pieces. Can't really do right now …"

"Blocked, eh?" And switching to a faked hysteria miming his friend: *"Buhuu – I'm depressed and can't work …"* Another refill.

"And yet you know how it works! Come up with an idea, write it down. And please, write it with your inner fucking critic switched off. You think to much, Shakespeare! You'll overload. But at least in that you are experienced, aren't you? Tell me: You two had a night back then?"

"Well, we had our climax, but then the tide was going out and left me stranded without anything to know. Just walked out of the room and left me. And stranded I still am."

"Taken any pills lately??? Mmhh. Okay then. Let's switch to cappuccino. Disgusting mixture – I know – but I think you'd better be sober."

III

What can I tell him? She did not want to think about his reaction yet, which she imagined being bitter. Was she able to take the rough with the smooth? Get over it? The fingers ran through the black hair as her bright grey eyes looked at the rain pelting down the streets, mirroring and blurring every light on the roads' surface.

The mechanically-driven voice announced the next stop. An elderly woman in the front part of the bus and two conspiratorial whispering boys sitting opposite the corridor, furtively glancing at her, rose and moved toward the exit. Was it her eyes that caught their attention? Cinnamon skin, a graceful body, her black hair embracing the dark lips and her piercing pale eyes. Finally the bus stopped and they got out. Still, it rained.

She had noticed him while sitting over a drink. He had been enthused in a chat with the barman. To her he had seemed like a regular, but she wasn't sure. He had ordered a BLT – a bacon, lettuce and tomato sandwich –, a cappuccino and a glass of tap water which had been brought to him after a little while. She remembered the funny expression every time he looked again at his scratch book notes and noticing a mistake, contradiction or a possible addition, erased, crossed out, added words with the swift and impatient movements of his black pen. Pleased with his writing he had looked up and around the bar, saw many couples and then … me. For an eternal second he had looked at her. He had finished eating and without any attempt to pay nodded towards the barkeeper and left. So he was, indeed, a regular and knew the barman damn well. She came to this very same bar the following days, fused by nothing better to do. There he was again. On the third evening he entered with a rucksack stuffed with several folders, a scrap book and an oversized book containing what? An anthology? He had already begun reading and making notes when she rose from her chair and headed for his table. She took the opposite chair, sat down while he lifted his brows and asked: *"So, what d'ya read?"*

Next station was announced. This one was hers. She got up and wrapped herself up in her coat.

IV

He hadn't seen her for weeks now. It must have been about two months already. Six weeks? Seven? The last time he had seen her he had been on the verge of exploding happiness, but now all he felt was betrayal rising inside his stomach, digging its vicious claws into his heart.

As if I don't have enough problems of my own. Actually, nothing did go as intended and desired. Now, what does she want? Why does she appear on board again? And his thoughts drifted away.

He simply could still not get it: This bunny was really telling him she was sorry. The worst-case scenario: though hurt still in love.

"SHUT THE FUCK UP, I ain't no heart to play vile games with! I can't take it! Just get out! "

"I said: *GET OUT, I DON'T WANT TO SEE YOU!!!"* And, moving closer until their eyes locked, his nose almost touching hers: *"I'm just not taking it!"*

As she listened to his spoken daggers flying, her eyes filled, tears rolled down her cheeks, smudging her mascara. He grabbed her by the arm and dragged her to the door, pushed her out, followed by a medley of fortissimo curses. Only when some of the other doors in the house opened, he stopped and stormed back inside his flat.

He slammed the door shut and, leaning against the closed door, sunk down. He was trapped in disbelief and tormented by thoughts. What can be done? Void. He vacillated between embracing love, hatred and utter contempt while he waited for the sounds of her stilletos' fading downstairs and the alarm of his pre-set timer.

Stiletto's fading? And it's seven alright … FUCK!!!

V

She rang at one of his neighbours; after some time an elderly voice crackled through the speaker and the door buzzed open. She did not remember on which floor his flat was, so she went to every door to look at the names. But after she finally found it, she hesitated, hesitated to ring and instead just sat down on the stairs. What if his reaction is worse than expected? If he doesn't let me explain? The whole thing? I'd better be going … She rose to her feet and with careful set steps attempted to leave the house. Having passed three steps already a door suddenly swung open and his voice appeared: *"C'mon in."* He left the door open, the flat's emerging light flooding the hall. Should I stay? Go?

VI

It is seven weeks already and she's really telling you how sorry she is? Show her that you're hurt man, with utter contempt arising!!! *"So, why did you leave?"* WHY DID YOU LEAVE??? Is that all? C'mon – you are hurt, badly hurt! She dragged your heart down the hotel's hallway that day, remember?! And you ask her: WHY DID YOU LEAVE?

"You didn't leave a note! What the heck was I supposed to think?! 'Yeah – she'll be back next fucking month?' Must have been amusing to think about what I was thinking that morning! So, you actually have a boy-friend? Had a boy-friend? A girl-friend?" Now, put in a more accusing node, raise your voice – insult her … "I don't believe this shit! You have neither one of them … Still you stood me up? Played 'catch me if you can – and you cannot'? You knew I had no chance with you! You know what? I don't want to hear any of your damn excuses. I want you to get out! Leave! NOW, GET OUT!!!" He grabbed her by the arm and dragged her to the door and pushed her out, slammed the door shut, and leaning against the closed door, sunk down. In the hallway he could hear her stilettos fading. One floor down, two floors down, main entrance door pulled open … .

In an energetic instant he rose, grabbed his pair of sneakers, grabbed his coat, the keys, his wallet – and stormed outside.

STATION [II 2006]

Time present and time past are
both perhaps present in time future
and time future contained in time past.
T. S. ELIOT

I

He now woke up. His tongue was slightly swollen and his mouth all dry. Which station? Did I miss mine? The crackling speakers' voice sprung to life and announced: *"Deterre. Next stop: Deterre!"* Deterre? Strange name. Can't remember that along the way. I'd better get off now.

This wagon was crowded, no seats were vacant, people stood shoulders to shoulders in the gangway, one arm stretched upwards to bars attached to the ceiling, the other holding the bags, suitcases and some careful packed instruments. Nobody could afford a loss. The stale air mixture of body sweat, cheap perfume and aftershave, gave headaches. Weary smiles exchanged whenever the train took a turn and people bumped against each other. After that each passenger tried hard to concentrate on events, great journeys, famous places mentioned in each traveller's guide. Anything not to think about this stale air, the oppressive confinement. The windows had already steamed up an eternal while ago. The numerous attempts at seeing something failed – wiping away the steam just lead to a kaleidoscope copy of the outside.

After some curves the train slowed down and came to a halt. The heavy metal doors swung open inwardly. The wagon emptied. All passengers got off. Finally he rose from his seat and walked towards the exit. Instead of taking each of the three steps down to the platform he jumped off the first one. He held his yellow bag – its brand's name already faded – with a tight grip in his left hand swung over his shoulder.

The station was illuminated with glaring white light from monotonously assembled fluorescent tubes hanging down from above the platform. This light was reflected by sterile white tiles covering both, the floor and the hall's wall. The hall itself was a huge tube. One part consisted of tracks, and still the train was passing through. The second part was just the platform.

This was the first underground railway station without any signs attached to the wall, no ticketing machines assembled, no docks. He looked both ways. Only people, their luggage to sit on or standing in the way.

II

"Hey there?! – Over here! Come on, want a coffee? My wife must still have some left ... I've seen you coming. What are you looking for? Lost something or someone?" asked an unknown voice along the way.

Frank stopped in an instant and looked to his right where he saw a couple and another guy sitting on their cases. *"No – err – thanks. Well, I thought that there might be an exit?! At either end of this station?"*

"Mmhh. What if I tell you that there might be none?"

"Pardon?"

"Excuse me. My name is Bud. This is Rose and that's Marc. We're here a bit longer than you'd expect us to be. And yet, we've found no exit so far ... Or did you come across any signs directing toward any 'exit'?"

"No ... actually not. But I've al ready wondered why there are no ads, no stickers on the wall – there's apparently no artists' underground scene down here. Everything just is so damn sterile ..."

"Still don't want a sip? Then sit down, join us."

"Well then," and with that he took the bag off his shoulder and sat down leaning his back against the cold tiled wall, *"how long have you been here?"*

"To be sincere: we don't know and I'm confused. I don't know anything about my whereabouts until I woke up in that damn train," Bud said.

"With me it's just the same ..."

"Everyone's quite puzzled," Marc exclaimed, *"nobody can remember where they' d intended to go. Against all odds nobody seems to have the faintest idea about where they come from,"* Marc explained. *"Pairing up in groups does not provide any new information, but it's better than being all alone."*

They fell silent once again, everyone of them indulging in their own secret thoughts, trying hard to make sense of their situation. Suddenly, Frank became aware of a girl to his right, leaning against the wall, being approached by an old man with a fatalistic gleam in his eyes. This man, his weight placed on a stick, stopped right in front of her, looked around and smiled contentedly.

"No one ever leaves the tunnel. We have to stay. We'll never leave – we'll never leave," he said while his right hand reached out for hers. She took some steps to the left and tried hard to hide her embarrassment and said *"Calm down. Easy, man. Just cool down, leave me alone!"*

Still, he would not let her go with it. He was closing in again.

"You know, little Miss – no light no life, so they say. Look around. What do you see? I see a station, tunnel, light, life. This tunnel is life, this train's time. No escape. Never escape a circle." Frank got up, approached him and grabbed his shoulder. *"Excuse me, mister. I don't mean to be rude, but you'd better be going. And thanks for letting us share in your secrets."*

***

"History and future seem to be extinct categories. I've already talked to the couple over there – with them it's the same. There's only a below-earth history," Marc announced. *"I'll be back in a minute. Just going for a walk ...,"* he said.

Right after Marc left, a guy who had stood near them for a while approached the train and got on.

"Hey – what's he up to?" asked Frank.

"Sometimes someone just can't take it any longer and just leaves," Rose replied. *"I don't know what's the use in all this waiting anyway. I guess, because all the others do it ..."*

"But why? How can he leave? Where's he going? We do not get any news, don't know where we are, what's going to happen – are in a timeless loop of nothing happening but there's a chance of getting some news. Sometime."

"They get sick of this endless waiting, I guess.

III

With a concerned look she was looking at her husband: *"Everything all right with you?" "Yeah, I'm fine. Breathing's just getting harder. Must be the disinfectant,"* he said again, knuckling down under the blow of another violent cough – grimacing with pain.

"Strange ... I smell it too, but have seen nobody so far cleaning the spot ... So, do we all end up like this? Who is f***ing poisoning us?!"

***

"Heavens," Rose cried, "we've got to go! You need help."

"Rose ... It's no good. Can't take it ... no more. Help me up – please – get me on the train ..."

"There must be someone ..." she said, running her hands through his hair, over his sweaty forehead and cheeks, eyes locking on his.

"No Rose, nobody ... can help ... nobody. Get me up ... please," his body thrilled with another cough. With his left arm around Rose's shoulder he stood up.

"Hey Frank – mind taking the cases?" Rose asked. With shambling feet, barely holding the weakened body's weight, they reached the train. It stopped and the doors opened. Nobody was getting off, the wagons were empty. Throngs of people were waiting to get on. When Bud finally got on, Rose turned around: "I'm going with him. Please give me the suitcases. Keep my bag. There's not much in it anyway: a bottle of water, something to read and what else? I forgot ..."

IV

"Now, only we are left." And with that he combed his fingers through her almond hair. The train slowed down again, the brakes shrieked. New people arrived and with them rumours were spreading. Rumours about the chosen. It was not clear who was the fount of the belief that people must be chosen by 'it', 'him' or whatever other higher force. Conspiring whispers could be heard from every group, filling each one of them with hope, with anger and with despair: A few would be spared, would remain ...

The order known was out of order. Coughs mixed with cries and a realization not to be for long anymore.

***

He dampened a cloth with the water that was still left, pressed it against his mouth, damped her spirits. It was just a matter of time. Breathing was getting harder – for him. Like the others he would end up coughing violently, running a temperature, sweating, getting weaker, spitting blood.

***

How do you know your train is due? Well, just take the last one available.

He felt her embrace from behind, noticed her whispering, deciphering the meaning without understanding the words. His time had come. She freed herself, gently pushed him a bit forward – just enough to raise herself. Then reaching under his arms her hands interlocked on his breast and she helped him up.

His head was heavy, his muscles sore. His back hurt – he could barely lift his bag. For a last time her hand passed across his face, wiping away the sweat on his forehead, moving it down and circling his beautiful lips. *"See you?"* he asked – his voice crackling. *"I'll take the next; if it's not too crowded. I love ..."* Without ending the last sentence her lips sealed his', her arms violently embracing, like she never wanted to go away again. Finally, she gave him free.

He stumbled to the train, dragged himself back up the three steps of the wagon. Once inside, the metal doors closed. His tongue was swelling, going numb. He wanted to wave her a good-bye. Instead, he passed out.

This is the way the world ends
Not with a bang but a whimper.
T. S. ELIOT